You are not just ordinary young men and women. You are choice spirits who have been held in reserve to come forth in this day. (For the Strength of Youth *[Salt Lake City: The Church of Jesus Christ of Latter-day Saints, 1990], p. 3)*

HOW TO BE AN
EXTRAORDINARY
TEENAGER

John Bytheway

Deseret Book is a registered trademark of Deseret Book Company.

Library of Congress Catalog Card Number 99-075202

ISBN 1-57345-607-1

Printed in the United States of America   72082-6602

10   9   8   7   6   5   4   3   2   1

*Being extraordinary is just being
ordinary with a little "extra."*

ORDINARY TEENS

want someone else
to make them happy

"Okay, world, listen up. Everyone out there dedicate yourself to making me happy." That's the attitude of ordinary teens. If they're not happy, someone is obviously not doing his or her job. It's their parents' fault, their teachers' fault, the principal's fault, the boss's fault, the government's fault, the weather's fault, the bad traffic's fault; it might even be the bed's fault (they got up on the wrong side of it). Nothing is *their* fault. It's all *someone else's* fault. If all those other folks out there would just get *their* act together, then maybe ordinary teens would be happy.

EXTRAORDINARY TEENS

know that happiness
is an inside-out job

Extraordinary teens know that the people in this world who are happy have just as many problems as the rest of us. They just *choose* to be happy anyway. They realize that they can't control all the circumstances *out there,* but they can control what's *in here,* or what's inside. Extraordinary teens are affected by all those outside things, but they're not infected by them. Extraordinary teens know that happiness is a choice, and they choose happiness every day.

ORDINARY TEENS
love to lounge

Hang out, hang around, sit around, do nothing. Ordinary teens know that this is the life. (Sigh.) Just relax and be a sofa spud. (Yawn.) They know that a lifetime of lounging will bring them the wonderful rewards of mediocrity, averageness, and ho-hummery. (Exhale.) That's okay. They're ordinary. Anything else would require getting up. And they're just too darn tired.

EXTRAORDINARY TEENS

love to learn

Extraordinary teens get excited about learning. Sure, lounging is easier, requires less energy, and has a certain appeal. But extraordinary teens have developed a taste for discovery. They may lounge for a minute or two, but not for very long. Eventually they rise from their comatose state, get off the couch, and get after life. They know that with each new bit of knowledge and experience, they will become more interesting, more fascinating, and more exciting. They see life as a perpetual treasure hunt, and the treasure they seek is knowledge.

ORDINARY TEENS
have a tendency toward television

Ordinary teens love television. Just pass them the remote and the cheese puffs, and don't walk in front of the set. It doesn't even matter what's on. Ordinary teens will channel-surf through filth, rubbish, slime, muck, and putrescence. Ordinary teens feel that they have to watch *something*. Not watching is out of the question. In fact, ordinary teens have been heard to say things like, "Mom, there's nothing else on!" (In other words, "I *have* to watch this. The only alternative would be not watching at all, and that's just not ordinary.")

EXTRAORDINARY TEENS

have a bias for books

Walt Disney said, "There is more treasure in books than in all the pirates' loot on Treasure Island . . . and best of all, you can enjoy these riches every day of your life!" Extraordinary teens know this. Books can take them wherever they want to go. And if the book gets trashy, they can easily put it down and find another one. They never have to say, "There's nothing else to read!" Cable or satellite may have more than 200 channels, but there are *millions* of books out there. And with a little thing called a library card, extraordinary teens can have their pick of any of them for free.

ORDINARY TEENS

try to become popular

Any ordinary teen knows that the goal of school is to see how many times you can get your picture to appear in the yearbook. School has very little to do with education. It has everything to do with climbing the social ladder and becoming popular. Ordinary teens know that they should let their popularity shine, so that people will glorify them. They worship the god of popular opinion, do what the popular people do, dress how the popular people dress, listen to the music that the popular ones listen to, in order to be like, so totally popular.

EXTRAORDINARY TEENS

try to become respected

Extraordinary teens live by what they know is true. If popularity comes their way, that's fine. But they don't seek after it. They seek the living God and try to live his gospel. They try to let their gospel light shine, so that others will see their good works and glorify their Father in heaven (see Matthew 5:16). They know it is much better to be respected than it is to be popular. Extraordinary teens know that popularity is temporary—it ends on yearbook day. But the gospel light is real and lasting and it will shine forever.

ORDINARY TEENS

want to make money

Bucks, dinero, mulah, dough. That's what it's all about, right? Whoever said money can't buy happiness doesn't know where to shop. Ordinary teens may believe that money and the things it can buy will make them happy. They think high net worth means high self-worth. More clothes, more CDs, more stuff! You bet. All they need is a stash of cash, and *then* they'll be happy.

EXTRAORDINARY TEENS

want to make a difference

Some people seem to have it all—fame, popularity, wealth—but they're still not happy. They haven't learned what extraordinary teens know, that the way to be happy is to forget about yourself, find someone who needs you, and make a difference in that person's life. Then, when your head hits the pillow at the end of the day, you can know that someone out there feels better tonight because you were there. Extraordinary teens know that at the end of their lives, they're not going to wish they had spent more time at the office. Instead, they'll be thinking about the people they love most, their family and friends, and hoping they made a difference.

ORDINARY TEENS

love to be with their friends

Of course people love to be with their friends. It's only ordinary. When you're with friends, you laugh, joke, drive around, and have fun. Some of the greatest memories people have of high school will be the times they spent with their friends. Ordinary teens define a friend as anyone who accepts them as they are. And ordinary people love to be with people who accept them.

EXTRAORDINARY TEENS
love to be a friend

Extraordinary teens also love to be with their friends. They love doing all the fun things as well. But they have a special definition of friends. A friend is someone who makes it *easier* to live the gospel of Jesus Christ (see Robert D. Hales, *Ensign,* May 1990, p. 40). Extraordinary teens want friends who accept them as they are, but they also choose friends who will inspire them to become more. Extraordinary teens are also friends to others. Their peer pressure is positive. People who hang out with extraordinary friends always come home wanting to be better.

ORDINARY TEENS

live in a house

Ordinary teens live with other people in a house. They have their own rooms, and they do their chores (after a few reminders and sometimes threats that they won't be able to take the Taurus). They have brothers and sisters who also live in the house, but they often fight and quarrel and cut each other down as they pass the peas. They won't let anyone come in their rooms or borrow their stuff. This is all fairly ordinary.

EXTRAORDINARY TEENS

live in a family

Extraordinary teens also live in a house. But they know that God sent them to be part of a family. Extraordinary teens know that when a bunch of people live together in a tight space, they are bound to bump into each other from time to time. But that's okay. They see their family as a team, all trying to get to the same place together. Extraordinary teens are wise enough to realize that with time, their parents and siblings will become some of the most important people in the world to them. They know that rude or harsh comments spoken in haste will be deeply regretted later in life, so they watch their tongues. Extraordinary teens reside in a house, but they live with their family.

ORDINARY TEENS
do what they're told

When ordinary teens have jobs, they do what they're told. If they're told to sweep the floor, they do it. If they're told to wipe off the counter, they do it. No big deal. When the boss is away, they relax a little and wait until he or she gets back so they'll know what to do next. They love their fifteen-minute breaks, and if they notice that something is wrong or needs to be done, they wait for the boss to come back and tell them what to do. You see, they're ordinary. They do what they're told, and they get the ordinary wage.

EXTRAORDINARY TEENS

do what they're told,
plus a little extra

Extraordinary teens may have the same jobs as ordinary ones. But if they're told to sweep the floor, they sweep it—plus a little extra. They also wipe off the counter if they're told, and then they do a little extra. When the boss is away, they say to themselves, What else needs to be done? And they do that little extra. They act like they own the place! They take personally what happens on the job, and they take pride in their work. They always do what they're told, plus a little extra. And they take home the ordinary wage, plus a little extra.

ORDINARY TEENS

try to be interesting

Ordinary teens hope that others will notice them. Every day they want to have something new to talk about. They want to be sure that they saw that movie on TV last night, because if someone says, "Hey, did you see that show last night?" they want to say, "Yeah, wasn't it good?" They want people to notice their nice clothes and their cool cars. They want to be popular. And that's only ordinary.

EXTRAORDINARY TEENS

try to be interested

Extraordinary teens aren't interested in being interesting. What interests them is being interested. They find that the best way to make friends is to be interested in other people and other things. Extraordinary teens ask lots of questions and then listen closely. And because they spend more time listening than talking, they end up learning a lot. Extraordinary teens know that there's nothing more interesting than a person who's interested. Isn't that interesting?

ORDINARY TEENS

want to be different

Ordinary teens want to be seen as individuals. They want to be recognized for their own uniqueness. Sometimes they go to great lengths to look different: different hair, different clothes, different styles. Some will even poke holes in their bodies in unusual places to be different. And then they'll find some other perforated friends who also want to be different and they'll all try to be different together although they look exactly the same. But it's normal. Lots of teens want to be different, just like everybody else.

EXTRAORDINARY TEENS

want to be valiant

Extraordinary teens are already aware of their own uniqueness. They want to be valued as individuals, but they also want to follow the ideal. Extraordinary teens don't ask, "What do I want to do?" they ask, "What *should* I do?" Extraordinary teens are not as focused on being *different* as they are on being *good*. And they soon discover that there's nothing more "different" than a teenager who wants to be valiant.

ORDINARY TEENS

think about their problems

Everyone has problems. And many ordinary people think about their problems all day long. They think about how they look, how they dress, how they talk. They wonder if they're smart; they wonder if anyone likes them. They spend so much time thinking about their problems, they don't have time to think about anything else! The only thing they use their imaginations for is a continuous acting-out of worst-case scenarios. When they ignore their blessings and look only at their burdens, the worst case is ordinarily what they get.

EXTRAORDINARY TEENS
think about their possibilities

Extraordinary teens realize that they have problems. But they'd rather spend their time thinking about their blessings. They realize that they can change the channel on their thoughts anytime they want! They're in charge of their own brains. So, instead of the faithless practice of problem pondering, they promptly pick the possibility program. "I know I have problems, but I also have gifts. What can I do? How can I give? What can I become?" Extraordinary teens use their imaginations to think about their possibilities—and they have the most extraordinary daydreams!

ORDINARY TEENS

hold on to grudges

Life's hard, and bad things are bound to happen to all of us. People make mistakes. They say or do things that offend others. People get hurt. That's part of life. When it happens to ordinary teens, they might hold a grudge. They let the angry feelings fester inside like a bad burrito. Holding on to the anger spoils everything else they're trying to do in life. This isn't just a problem for teens. Ordinary adults also carry around grudges as if they had value. Some are still upset that their Aunt Mabel didn't come to their wedding breakfast in 1967. It still bugs them. But, oh well. That's just the way ordinary people are.

EXTRAORDINARY TEENS

let go and forgive

Extraordinary teenagers learn to forgive. They hand their problems over to God and let him sort out the justice and mercy. Life's a lot easier that way. Extraordinary teens know that if they don't forgive, they burn the bridge over which they themselves must pass! They realize that they need forgiveness too, so they pray for the power to be forgiving. They don't want to be bitter; they want to be better! In especially tough cases, they remember that God has *extra*ordinary power, and sometimes, when we ask, he shares it with us so we can forgive and let go.

ORDINARY TEENS

obey because they have to

Ask ordinary teens why they go to church or keep the standards, and they might reply, "Because my mom makes me," or "My dad would kill me if I didn't." They follow the rules because they have to. To them, the Church is just one long set of rules designed to make sure they don't have any fun. They focus on the movies they can't see, the dates they can't go on until they're older, and the clothes they can't wear. They say, "I *have* to do this, and I *have* to do that." No wonder they're miserable. And ordinary. They have to be.

EXTRAORDINARY TEENS

obey because they want to

Extraordinary teens have already learned that the way to be happy is to live the "plan of happiness." They have no interest in breaking the rules because they know they will only break themselves in the process. To them, obedience isn't an irritation, it's a quest! They're excited about how they've chosen to live. They know they're going without some things, but they focus on what they do have. They think of the movies they can see, the dates they can go on someday, and the clothes they can wear. They say, "I *get* to do this, and I *get* to do that." They have peace of conscience and a feeling of happiness that those who resist the rules don't understand. They know that the standards may be tough, but they're true! So what else matters?

ORDINARY TEENS

are happy when they succeed

Ordinary teens love to win. They're happy when they win a trophy, ace a test, or make a tough shot. Of course they are: that's ordinary! But some ordinary teens see success as a pie with only so many slices. If someone else wins, it takes away part of their prize. They love to win, but they feel threatened if others win. They're happy when they succeed, but when others succeed, they look only at themselves. And they often feel they've fallen short.

EXTRAORDINARY TEENS

are happy when others succeed

Extraordinary teens love to see others win. They know that success never runs out. Success isn't just one pie, it's a twenty-four-hour perpetual pie factory. They love to see their friends do well. Whenever someone else wins, Success just bakes another pie. Extraordinary teens go out to celebrate with their successful friends, and they supply the Cool Whip.

ORDINARY TEENS

want to look good

Each morning, after they rub the sleep from their eyes, take a shower, and get dressed, ordinary teens face the mirror. They want to look good, and that's ordinary. The sign on their fridge says, "You are what you eat." They want their clothes to be nice, their hair to shimmer just right in the light, and their car to project just the right image—something new, cool, and fast, or anything with big tires and a roll bar. For ordinary teens, image is everything.

EXTRAORDINARY TEENS

want to be good

Extraordinary teens want to look good too. But they're concerned with something extra. They wish they had another mirror in the morning that they could look in to see if their spirit is healthy. The sign on their fridge says, "You are what you watch, listen to, read, and think about." Fresh clothes and a neat appearance are important, but they want to be spiritually dressed as well. Extraordinary teens know that ordinary people look at outside things, but the Lord looks on the heart. For extraordinary teens, image is nice, but nothing looks as good as being good.

ORDINARY TEENS
ask, "What do I get?"

Ordinary teens want to know, "What's in it for me?" There must be an incentive. "I'll go to the service project if the girls are coming," says the ordinary young man. If it's hard or inconvenient, ordinary teens suddenly remember they have other plans. Like the six-year-old on Christmas morning, they are most concerned with what they might get. To be sure, focusing only on getting will eventually get them something—a rather empty, hollow feeling, accompanied by the questions, "Is that all there is? Is there anything else?"

EXTRAORDINARY TEENS

ask, "What can I give?"

Extraordinary teens "get it." They understand that the empty feeling that comes with always wanting more can be replaced by the filled-up feeling of giving more than they get. So instead of asking, "What do I get out of this?" they focus on what they can add to it. They make their family, their friends, their ward, and everything they're involved in better because they focus on what they can give. They understand the lesson from the talking little stream, "Wherever I go, the *grass grows greener* . . ." Like the little stream, extraordinary teens have learned to give away.

ORDINARY TEENS

complain

🌵

There's always something to complain about when you're ordinary. An ordinary teen can look around the room right now and find five things to complain about in five seconds: "My room is too small, my clothes don't fit, my friends get to do fun things, I have more jobs than anyone, my mom thinks this book will make me extraordinary." Yeah, yeah, yeah, ordinary teens know that the whole world has conspired to make sure they don't have any fun. Ordinary teens have developed ordinary eyesight that enables them to see problems wherever they look. And eventually, they complain so much that they become a part of the problem.

EXTRAORDINARY TEENS

contribute

Extraordinary teens are not blind to their problems. They see them, but their extraordinary vision enables them to see more. Inside every problem, they see an opportunity to contribute. Abe Lincoln (whom we would call extraordinary) said, "He has the right to criticize who has the heart to help." Extraordinary teens find a way to solve the problem. Some problems, however, are more than even extraordinary teens can handle. When that happens, they remember that for every math book full of problems, there is a Teacher's Edition full of solutions. They know they can go to the Master Teacher and ask for help.

ORDINARY TEENS

waste time

Ordinary teens have a daily "to-do" list. Items one through ten say *Hang around*. This is especially true in the summer when school's out. Sleep in, watch TV, guzzle pop, take a nap (not necessarily in that order). These are all very worthwhile activities for ordinary teens. And after three months of such activity, look what they have to show for it! When they go back to school and friends ask, "What did you do this summer?" they say, "Well, um, let's see, I inhaled, exhaled, and pumped blood for three months."

EXTRAORDINARY TEENS

make time count

Extraordinary teens know there's more to life than being lifeless. Their daily "to-do" list includes entries like *walk, run, hike, fish, bike, sing, mow, weed, paint, read, write, draw, serve, grow, live, learn, laugh,* and *play.* Just reading their list would make ordinary teens want another nap. Extraordinary teens know that time is a luxury, and they live life at the top of their lungs! When they go back to school and friends ask, "What did you do this summer?" they say, "What did I *do?* What *didn't* I do! I had an *extraordinary* summer. You can read about it in volumes 68, 69, and 70 of my journal."

ORDINARY TEENS
get bored

"There's nothing to do" is a typical quote from an ordinary teenager. Ordinary teens sometimes expect life to be a four-star, two-thumbs-up roller coaster of action, adventure, and romance accompanied by an Oscar-winning soundtrack in THX Dolby Surround Sound. It isn't. So they sit around feeling dull, acting dull, looking dull, and wondering why life is so dull. If they tell their parents, "There's nothing to do," Mom hands them a list of chores, and Dad tells how when he was sixteen he had to build a small college with his bare hands to earn fifteen cents. Now they have a list with more work to do, but they're still bored. Their ordinary brains can't think of a thing.

EXTRAORDINARY TEENS

get busy

Extraordinary teens know that being bored is a luxury. Being bored is just another way of saying, "I have the chance to do anything I want." Extraordinary teens have so many things they'd love to do, they have trouble choosing what they're going to do! They realize that one day they will have barely enough time to do what they *have* to, let alone what they *want* to. So anytime they're tempted to get bored, they just get excited, and then they get busy.

ORDINARY TEENS

are cordial

Ordinary teens are nice. They haven't thought about manners very often, but they are, you know, nice. When they go over to a friend's house, they enter the room in a slouch while jawing their gum. "Is Cheryl here?" they mutter in library tones as they examine the carpet. Ordinary teens rarely lift their eyes above doorknob level when talking to their friends' parents. While waiting, ordinary teens resume their slouch on the couch, glance at a magazine, and watch the dog scratch. Gee, that's nice. Nice and ordinary.

EXTRAORDINARY TEENS

are classy

When extraordinary teens enter a room, the place lights up like Temple Square at Christmas. "Hi, Mrs. Taylor! How are you?" they ask with youthful energy and a handshake. "Great, Eddy, how are you?" Mrs. Taylor echoes with enthusiasm she didn't know she had until Eddy showed up. "I'm fine, thanks. Hey, I've come to pick up Cheryl. Is she ready?" "Sure, I'll tell her you're here—would you like to sit down?" (Extraordinary teens would never take a seat unless invited.) When Cheryl's dad walks in, extraordinary teens stand up, shake hands, and speak to him eye to eye. Even the golden retriever wags his tail knowing there's someone extraordinary in the room (dogs can sense things like that). Ordinary teens behave in an ordinary manner. But extraordinary teens have extraordinary manners.

ORDINARY TEENS

are discontented

Ordinary teens don't know why, but they're never quite content. They want to be happy all the time, but they're not. They seem to be stuck in a bad mood. When another problem comes along, they think that something's wrong with them or wrong with life. They can't figure out why the Problem Fairy makes such frequent stops under their pillow. They think that life isn't supposed to be like this. They are quite sure they have more problems than anyone else.

EXTRAORDINARY TEENS

are discovering

Extraordinary teens are aware that life is a never-ending series of problems, and that it's supposed to be that way. Happy times are great, but never permanent (not in this life, anyway). Extraordinary teens have discovered that every problem they live through makes them stronger. Every challenge reveals something new about them that they get to discover. They remember that they've learned the most in life not from their easy times but from their hardest times.

ORDINARY TEENS

watch television

There is nothing wrong with filling up your mind with television. In fact, it's quite ordinary. (It's also ordinary for a trash compactor to be filled up with garbage.) Television is a brilliant invention that can be used as a tool or a weapon. Ordinary teenagers use it for some of both. It's ordinary to watch other people live their dreams and get rewarded with fame, popularity, and mulah. It's also ordinary to idle away time, even though we've been told, "Thou shalt not idle away thy time" (D&C 60:13).

EXTRAORDINARY TEENS

watch their own vision

Extraordinary teens may watch a decent TV program once in a while—but not for the ordinary 3.25 hours per day. They're not content with sitting in a thoughtless stupor and watching other people live their dreams. Extraordinary teens have their own dreams. They feel that their own lives, missions, and destinies are more important to them than the lives of overpaid TV stars or athletes whom they'll probably never meet. They have their own vision of what they'd like to become, and extraordinary teens know they'll never achieve it by watching television. They know that time spent watching TV is prime time to work on their dreams.

ORDINARY TEENS

know what to do

Ordinary teens know what to do. They believe that knowledge is power. They know all about being brave, clean, and reverent, and about faith, divine nature, and individual worth. They know the Ten Commandments, and they do well at scripture chase. In fact, ordinary teens may know several Primary songs *by heart*. Wow. It's good to know things, but it's only ordinary. The athletic shoe company would have only ordinary sales if its slogan was "just know it."

EXTRAORDINARY TEENS

do what they know

Extraordinary teens believe that knowledge is power, but they also realize that knowledge is powerless without action. So not only do they *know* what to *do,* they actually *do* what they *know.* They remember that the words to the Primary song were changed from "teach me all that I must *know*" to "teach me all that I must *do*" (*Hymns,* no. 301). They try to put what they know into action. They strive, struggle, stumble, and stretch. Extraordinary teens know what they need to know, but they take it a step further and "just do it."

ORDINARY TEENS

react

Ever hear of Pavlov's dog? He's almost as famous as Lassie. A guy named Pavlov would ring a bell and then give his dog some meat. Pretty soon, every time the dog heard the bell, he would salivate because he knew it was Alpo time. Scientists got really excited about this and wrote lots of books and articles. What does this have to do with teenagers? Sit. Stay. And I'll explain. Some teenagers, ordinary teenagers, react. When something happens, they don't think about their response, they just react. If someone's rude to them, they get mad. They use phrases like "He makes me so mad," as if "he" had complete control over their reactions. And if they're ordinary, perhaps "he" does.

EXTRAORDINARY TEENS

respond

Extraordinary teens don't react, they respond. They understand that they can choose *how* they react. They know they can control their responses to things like bells and rude boys. Pavlov's dog was ordinary. His canine brain couldn't say, "I know I just heard a bell, but this time, I'm going to trick that pesky master of mine and not let my mouth water. I think I'll roll over and chase an R.V." Dogs can't choose their responses. Human beings can. They have the *ability* to *respond*. We call it response-ability. When bad things happen to extraordinary teens, they know that they get to choose how they will respond. They can even "turn the other cheek," choosing to do the opposite of what their initial "reaction" would be. *This* is being extraordinary.

ORDINARY TEENS
bring problems to the boss

   Ordinary teens make ordinary employees. If something goes wrong, they run to the boss and say, "What should we do?" Reporting problems is a good thing to do, but it is rather ordinary. Now the boss has to sit there and ask more questions and come up with a solution. (This gives him less time to choose who gets the coveted "Employee of the Month" plaque with the $2 Baskin Robbins coupon.) The boss doesn't feel like he can go anywhere because all of the employees need his problem-solving abilities. By themselves, his employees wouldn't know what to do. You know why? They're ordinary.

EXTRAORDINARY TEENS

bring solutions to the boss

Extraordinary teens are great employees. If something goes wrong, they think of several possible solutions and bring them to the boss. If they don't have time to go to the boss, or if the boss isn't there, they try to solve the problem on their own and then tell the boss what they did as soon as he returns. Now the boss knows that he can leave whenever he needs to, because he's got an extraordinary teen minding the store. Extraordinary teens know that the best way to get a raise or some more responsibility is to solve their boss's problems. (And what about the coveted "Employee of the Month" plaque with $2 Baskin Robbins coupon? It's in the bag.)

ORDINARY TEENS

go to church

Ordinary teens get up each Sunday morning 'cause that's what they ordinarily do. They pick out some clothes and head for the chapel. Ordinary teens leave their scriptures home because, well, they're heavy. When they get to the chapel, they rest their craniums on the bench in front of them or draw pictures during the talks. They mess around and whisper to their friends. Later, if the couch in the foyer isn't available, they might eventually end up in Sunday School. Ordinary teens have a hard time focusing on the lesson, though, so they continue to mess around with their friends. If they need to "get a drink," they just get up and leave. It's ordinary.

EXTRAORDINARY TEENS

go to worship

♡

Extraordinary teens go to worship. They look in the closet and say, "What should I wear?" Then they ask themselves, "What does God deserve?" and they make their choice. Extraordinary teens don't need to rest their heads on the bench because they got enough sleep the night before. They listen to each speaker and teacher; they know how hard it is to give a talk and see people ignoring you or talking and being rude. They came to be taught by the Spirit, and they know that no matter who the speaker is, they can be inspired and edified if they're in tune. Extraordinary teens don't go to church because it's fun. They go to worship.

ORDINARY TEENS

talk about others

When ordinary teens get together, one of their favorite topics is other teens. They talk about what other people did, what other people said, or what they think other people are. It's easier to talk about other people behind their backs than in front of their backs. Ordinary teens notice that a strange kind of bonding occurs when they all gang up and talk about someone else. But "gossip glue" is bad bonding—because ordinary teens have to wonder who the group talks about when they're not there. Maybe it's them.

EXTRAORDINARY TEENS

talk about ideas

Extraordinary teens know that small minds talk about people, mediocre minds talk about things, and great minds talk about ideas. Extraordinary teens love to talk to their friends. But they'd rather not talk *about* their friends. If the conversation turns to a friend who isn't there, their behind-the-back talk is always positive. Extraordinary teens prefer to talk about ideas, plans, goals, and dreams. They love to talk about what they learned in seminary, or what new idea they had about life. They often lose track of time because they're so excited about what they've discovered. When others start to gossip, extraordinary teens say, "I have an idea; let's talk about ideas."

ORDINARY TEENS

ask, "Why did this happen?"

Life is hard for everyone at times. Ordinary teens can't understand why they have trials and problems. They ask, "Why me?" They may think that life isn't supposed to be so hard. They may say things like, "I didn't deserve this," or, "I've been doing what I'm supposed to, so why did this happen?" They may even think that life has singled out their family to receive the most problems.

EXTRAORDINARY TEENS

ask, "What can I learn?"

🦎

Extraordinary teens also have problems. They recognize that bad things happen to good people. They remember that Abraham, Nephi, Abinadi, John the Baptist, Joseph Smith, and even Jesus all received trials they didn't deserve. They know that life is a series of tests, trials, temptations, and even tragedies. Extraordinary teens go humbly to the Lord and ask, "What lessons can I learn, and how can I grow from this experience?" Their trials push them closer to the Lord, not further away. They discover that within every trial is the opportunity to become more submissive, charitable, forgiving, and patient. They remember the words from "How Firm a Foundation" (*Hymns,* no. 85): "The flame shall not hurt thee; I only design thy dross to consume and thy gold to refine."

ORDINARY TEENS

follow the crowd

Ordinary teens want to know where everyone's going so they can follow them there. (Baaaa.) What's everyone wearing these days? (Mooo.) What's everyone watching? (Oink-oink-oink.) Once they find their crowd, they want to be like them. (Quack-quack-quack.) What should they wear? *Follow the crowd.* Style of their hair? *Follow the crowd.* Movies to see? *Follow the crowd.* Newest CD? *Follow the crowd.* Ordinary teens haven't noticed yet that following the crowd gets crowded. Lots of people, but no direction! And more important, no director.

EXTRAORDINARY TEENS
follow the Creator

Extraordinary teens follow the Creator. They remember that in Bethlehem there were two groups—the inn crowd and the stable few. The crowd may lead them many places, but only the Creator can change their hearts, forgive their sins, give them peace, and bring them home. They know that the Lord can make a lot more out of their lives than they can (see Ezra Taft Benson, *Ensign,* December 1988, p. 4). Sure, there are lots of questions about music, movies, and concerts. But the questions about "where to go" are answered when you know "whom to follow." Extraordinary teens follow the Creator.

ORDINARY TEENS

take the sacrament

Ordinary teens go to church. They find their usual spot on the bench and they sit. They sit through the announcements and the ward business. They sit through the sacrament hymn and the sacrament prayer. When the tray comes down their row, someone nudges them so they'll take the sacrament and pass it on. Then they resume their normal activity of dozing or drawing or doing nothing. What do you expect? They're ordinary.

EXTRAORDINARY TEENS

make covenants

Extraordinary teens go to Church to worship. They love being in a ward family. They smile and shake a lot of hands as they come in. They listen during the business and announcements. They sing the sacrament hymn and pay attention to the words. And when the tray comes down their row, they take the sacrament and make a covenant. Extraordinary teens think about what it means to take upon them the name of Jesus. They know they're facing another week of school where they must stand as witnesses of God at all times, in all things, and in all places. They know others will be watching them. They ponder what they'll have to do this week so they may always have His spirit to be with them. Extraordinary teens know it's not enough to remember Him only on Sunday. They know they've made a covenant to *always* remember Him.

ORDINARY TEENS
pray for luck

When ordinary teens see others accomplish goals, they may say, "Wow. They're so lucky!" They think a person who can play the piano or paint a picture was just lucky to have gotten that talent. So they resume their daily activity of hanging out and watching TV and wondering why others get all the breaks. They gather four-leaf clovers, horseshoes, and rabbit's feet as if they had some kind of power. They hope that when opportunity knocks, they'll be lucky enough to get the door. People who hate to prepare will tell you—success is a matter of luck.

EXTRAORDINARY TEENS

prepare for opportunity

Extraordinary teens know that opportunity doesn't knock, really. People create opportunity by being prepared. "Luck" is when preparation meets opportunity. In other words, the opportunity comes along, and only the prepared can take it! As the old saying goes, "The harder I practice, the luckier I get!" Extraordinary teens would rather work than wish. They know that when you see a man on top of a mountain, you can bet he didn't fall there.

ORDINARY TEENS
stick to the script

Ordinary teens know just how to "act." They figure out what part they want to play, and they follow the script. If they're popular, then they act the way they think popular people act. If they're athletes or jocks, then they act the way they think athletes or jocks act. Sometimes that may mean being unkind or cliquish, but they do it anyway, because it's in the script! And ordinary teens are scripted. If you ask ordinary teens where the script comes from, they're not sure. Ordinary teens act the way they do because, well, that's the way others have acted, or that's the way they act on TV shows named after zip codes.

EXTRAORDINARY TEENS

stick to the scriptures

Extraordinary teens are eager to know what part they can play. They follow a script too. It tells them exactly how they should act. When you ask them where their script came from, they're sure. In fact, they have another name for their scripts—*sure* scripts, or scriptures. Sure scripts come from a better source than Hollywood or the halls of school. Sure scripts have been around a long time, and they show extraordinary people how they should act. Extraordinary teens wouldn't be part of the act if the script was bad, so they make sure their script is sure.

ORDINARY TEENS

make excuses

Ordinary teens can make excuses as fast as McDonald's makes fries. Billions and billions served. "I'm too tired, it's too hot, I'm not a morning person, he made me mad, I didn't have time, I'm an Aquarius." When something difficult is asked of ordinary teens, they cook up a large order of excuses for why it can't be done. When a certain father asked his oldest sons to retrieve some plates of brass, he received a rather ordinary response: "It is a hard thing you have required of us" (1 Nephi 3:5). Or, in other words, "Behold. We're ordinary."

EXTRAORDINARY TEENS

make tracks

Extraordinary teens don't make excuses, they just ask if they can be excused. Then they make tracks to accomplish the thing they've been asked. Extraordinary teens see stepping stones where ordinary teens see stumbling blocks. They know that success comes in cans, not in can'ts. They'd rather give out than give up. When a certain father asked his youngest son to retrieve some plates of brass, he answered, "I will go and do . . ." (1 Nephi 3:7). Then this extraordinary young man just went and did. He didn't make excuses; he just made tracks.

ORDINARY TEENS

have remote control

It's easy to push the buttons of ordinary teens. That's because they give away the remote to their feelings. They say things like, "He makes me so mad" or "She drives me crazy." If someone walking down the hall doesn't say "hi," ordinary teens act as if someone just pointed a remote at them and pushed "be depressed." Ordinary teens ride an emotional roller coaster because other people are always pushing their buttons. Anyone can program an ordinary teen's feelings—by remote control.

EXTRAORDINARY TEENS

have self-control

Extraordinary teens control themselves. They understand that "he" and "she" will always be out there doing different things. But extraordinary teens push their own buttons. They're not controlled by others. Not even remotely. They keep their control inside. They realize that the things others do may influence them but not control them. They can channel their feelings, lower the volume of outside voices, or mute them altogether. They have the power. They hold their own remote.

ORDINARY TEENS

think that seeing is believing

Ordinary teens want evidence before they'll make a change. They want to get paid before doing the work! They say things like, "If I had a stronger testimony, *then* I'd start saying my prayers every day," and "If Heavenly Father would just give me more spiritual experiences, *then* I'd study my scriptures." It's an ordinary attitude, but it's backwards when it comes to spiritual things. It's like saying to your fireplace, "Give me heat and then I'll give you wood."

EXTRAORDINARY TEENS

know that believing is seeing

Extraordinary teens make changes before they see the evidence. They've noticed that Jesus never said, "Because you have *seen,* now you'll have *faith.*" Instead, Jesus said, "Because of thy *faith,* thou hast *seen.*" They understand that faith precedes the miracle. Extraordinary teens are diligent in their prayers and scripture study not because they've seen, but because they believe. And extraordinary teens believe that someday, in the Lord's own way and time, they will see.

ORDINARY TEENS

listen to their peers

Ordinary teens try to listen to everyone talking at once. *Glamour* and *Seventeen* tell them what prom dresses to wear, *Entertainment Tonight* tells them what movies to see, and the chatter in the halls of school tells them who's dating who. Faithfully following peers is exhausting. And if ordinary teens follow their peers wherever they go, they'll be forced to make a series of compromises that may take them exactly where they're going: nowhere.

EXTRAORDINARY TEENS

listen to the prophets

Extraordinary teens know that above all the competing voices of the world, there is the gentle but uncompromising voice of a prophet. Extraordinary teens know that no one ever achieved their best by following the rest. Sure, they listen to their peers, but the deciding vote is always cast by the prophet. They hear all the other voices but they only hearken to one. In loving but powerful ways, a prophet's voice provides extraordinary teens with answers to life's big questions, and even a few of the little ones, like prom dresses to wear, movies to see, and how and whom to date. So for strength in their youth, extraordinary teens listen to the prophet's voice.

ORDINARY TEENS

want to know when Christ will come

Ordinary teens are interested in the topic of the Second Coming. They wonder about the signs of the times. Sometimes they worry about what's going to happen. They're aware of some of Satan's lies, like, "There is no devil," "There is no hell," and "There's no need to repent." But there's another lie that's so subtle and so clever that many ordinary teens have been fooled by it: *"There's no hurry."* Ordinary teens might say, "Someday I'll really study," or "Someday I'll really improve my prayers." There's only a hurry if the Second Coming is near.

EXTRAORDINARY TEENS

want to come unto Christ

Extraordinary teens are looking forward to when Christ will come, because they've already come unto Christ. They enjoy the blessings of the gospel right now, because they've jumped in with both feet. Extraordinary teens don't have to wonder, "Should I go to church or not?" "Should I get into seminary or not?" or "Should I keep the standards or not?" They've already chosen to follow the Savior, and they're in it for the long haul. Extraordinary teens know that the only way to feel peace about the Second Coming is to hurry and make the major decision of life: Come unto Christ.

ABOUT THE AUTHOR

John Bytheway was born and raised in Salt Lake City. He served a mission to the Philippines and later graduated from Brigham Young University. The author of numerous books and talk tapes, including the best-selling *What I Wish I'd Known in High School,* John is also a sought-after speaker and a part-time instructor in Religious Education at BYU. He and his wife, Kimberly, and their daughter, Ashley, live in Provo, Utah.